among
the
cypress

among the cypress

Photography by Gary Geiger

Text by Douglas Long

THE MONTEREY PENINSULA

GRAPHIC ARTS CENTER PUBLISHING®

International Standard Book Number 1-55868-091-8
Library of Congress Number 92-70124
© MCMXCII by Graphic Arts Center Publishing Company
P.O. Box 10306 • Portland, Oregon 97210
No part of this book may be reproduced by any means
without the permission of the publisher.
The photographs on pages 128 and 134 are
© MCMXCI and © MCMXC respectively by
Monterey Bay Aquarium, and are used by permission
We wish to thank Jeffers Literary Properties for permission
to reprint part of the poem "Tamar" by Robinson Jeffers.
President • Charles M. Hopkins
Editor-in-Chief • Douglas A. Pfeiffer
Managing Editor • Jean Andrews
Designer • Robert Reynolds
Cartographer • R. R. Donnelley
Typographer • Harrison Typesetting, Inc.
Book Manufacturing • Lincoln & Allen Co.
Printed in the United States of America
Third Printing

To Wendy, Sean, and Brett
— *Gary Geiger*

◄ ◄ Monterey cypress overlook the fourteenth hole at Cypress
Point Golf Course. This course, designed by Allistair MacKenzie,
was opened in 1928. Among the golfers it has challenged are
Presidents Eisenhower, Kennedy, and Ford. ◄ The twists and
gnarls of a dead Monterey cypress at Point Lobos show the harsh-
ness of salt air and severe winds. ► Sycamore leaves add autumn
color to Carmel Valley. ► ► At the eighth hole at Pebble Beach
Golf Links, a slice off the tee can drive the ball into the surf.

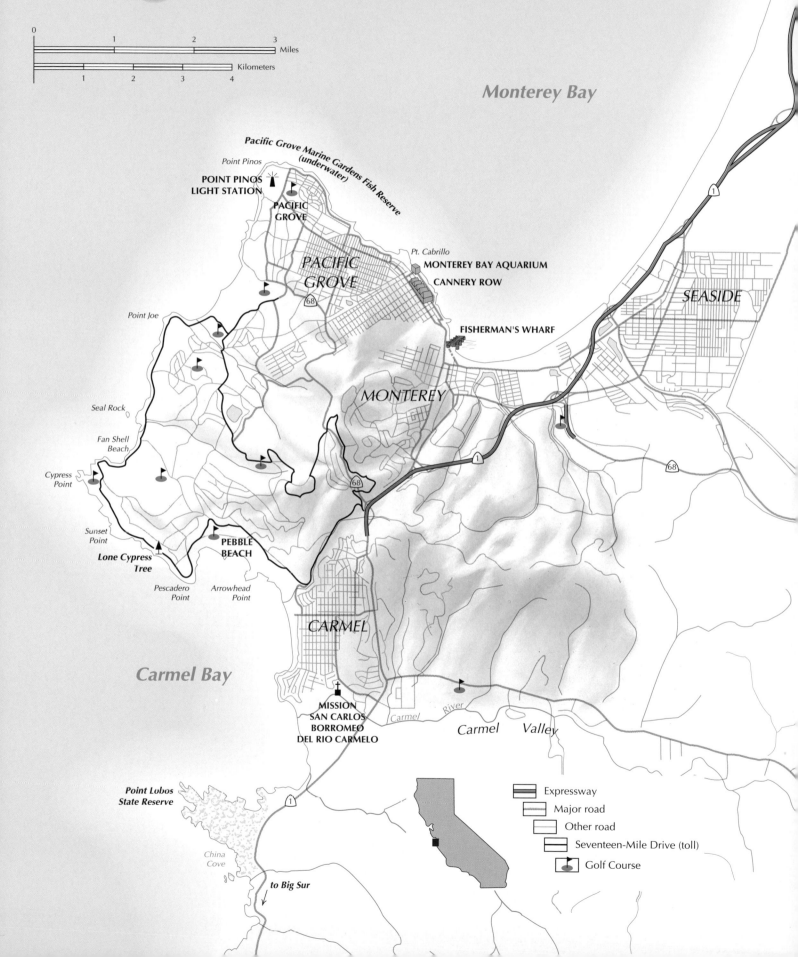

Monterey Bay

0   1   2   3
Miles

1   2   3   4
Kilometers

Pacific Grove Marine Gardens Fish Reserve
(underwater)

Point Pinos

**POINT PINOS
LIGHT STATION**

**PACIFIC
GROVE**

*PACIFIC
GROVE*

Pt. Cabrillo

MONTEREY BAY AQUARIUM

CANNERY ROW

Point Joe

68

FISHERMAN'S WHARF

SEASIDE

Seal Rock

MONTEREY

Fan Shell
Beach

Cypress
Point

1

68

Sunset
Point

**PEBBLE
BEACH**

**Lone Cypress
Tree**

Pescadero
Point

Arrowhead
Point

CARMEL

Carmel Bay

**MISSION
SAN CARLOS
BORROMEO
DEL RIO CARMELO**

River

Carmel

Carmel Valley

**Point Lobos
State Reserve**

1

*China
Cove*

Expressway

Major road

Other road

Seventeen-Mile Drive (toll)

Golf Course

to Big Sur

HISTORICAL OVERVIEW

On a warm and sunny morning in California's Carmel Valley, a five-minute drive in the direction of the coast can bring a drop in temperature of ten to twenty degrees, with enough fog and drizzle to require the turning on of headlights. At the mouth of the valley and southward toward Point Lobos and Big Sur, there might be nothing but a gray density of rolling mist. Turning northward onto Highway 1 and driving up the hill to Carmel could be a drive through a chilly cloud.

At Pebble Beach, the rare pine and cypress forest could be dripping and cool and dark. Yet head northward a mile or so to the coast at Pacific Grove, and suddenly the sun could be out, and at the harbor in Monterey, too, it might be a warm and pleasant day. There is possibly no other place on earth with the variety of climate and terrain that exists in the region of the Monterey Peninsula. The diversity here, from the valley to the mountains, from the forests to the ocean shore, is stunning to behold, and people have been attracted to it since time immemorial.

Scientists speculate that about fifteen thousand years ago human beings crossed the Bering Straits on a land bridge from Siberia to Alaska. Their descendants fanned southward, generation by generation, ultimately populating the Americas. It could be speculated further—with some degree

---

◀ The famous Lone Cypress clings to the granite near Midway Point along the 17-Mile Drive. This tree is *the* landmark on the Monterey Peninsula.

of certainty, though not exactly scientifically—that those who settled around the Monterey Peninsula had a discriminating eye for scenic beauty and an epicurean sense of what was good to eat. Here, within a fairly compact domain, they found spectacular mountains, lush valleys, scenic rivers, and the dramatic shore. And available for the taking were abalone, mussels, quail, pheasant, duck, deer, rabbit, elk, berries, roots, tubers, seeds, nuts—pine nuts were a staple—and a dazzling array of saltwater and freshwater fish. Whatever the season, there was always more than enough to eat.

These first people lived in small villages loosely connected with neighboring villages by kinship and language. Their dwellings were huts made of branches, and frequently, when the village trash heap grew too large or too ripe, they simply burned their huts down and rebuilt elsewhere. In summer, they built their villages near the shore. In winter, to escape the seaside cold and dampness, they built their villages inland.

For clothing, they wore capes and jackets made of animal hides. Adult women also wore skirts made of reeds in a fashion suggesting Polynesian grass skirts.

The Natives were, as an explorer described their kinsmen up the coast, ". . . a people of tractable, free and loving nature, without guile or treachery." Engaging in loud arguments or in strenuous wrestling was as close as they came to engaging in war, and it was extremely rare that anyone was ever killed. Sickness was virtually unknown. There was no hunger, poverty, or crime. For thousands of years, they lived this simple, healthy life. But their way of life, and they themselves, came to an abrupt end.

Since 1588, when the Spanish Armada was raked and crippled by the English fleet in the Channel and then reduced to piles of splinters by storms along the Irish coast, the Spanish had consistently lost wars, which in turn had cost them territory and influence. The only place they held their own and turned a tidy profit was in the Americas. From here sailed galleons, which were filled with silver and gold to brace up the Spanish treasury.

Then, in the 1760s, the Spanish became nervous about the Russians. Alarming letters were sent to Madrid from the Spanish ambassador in St. Petersburg expressing his fear and belief that the Russians were up to no good in the Americas. The Spanish Crown had better take notice and do something about it.

For years, Russians had explored the Alaskan coast and the Aleutian Islands. Lately, it seemed they actually intended to establish settlements there, which meant they could easily probe southward into the unoccupied Spanish territory of California and establish an outpost along that coast, perhaps threaten Mexico itself. The possibilities were unnerving. Russian intentions were yet unclear, but Catherine II was an extremely ambitious Czarina, just the type to horn in on the Spanish anywhere she thought she could get away with it.

Nor was she the only one casting a covetous eye. Looming forever in the forefront of Spanish consciousness were the English. They were a pesky bunch, always a threat. It had for some time been a concern of the Spanish that the English might sneak into California, establish bases, and raid southward. Two hundred years earlier, the wily, notorious plunderer, Sir Francis Drake, had made

himself a scourge, burning and looting numerous ports of New Spain. He also explored California's coast. Who knew what navigational charts the English might possess from Drake's time? And who could say what the English might do with them? Since 1763, when the English won their war with France and gained all the French territory in North America, the English had shared a border with the Spanish in the Mississippi Valley.

All in all, the Spanish felt vulnerable and threatened. It was time for them to act, or, more accurately, to react. They decided to establish outposts to fortify the coast of Upper California. They began at San Diego and Monterey.

On June 3, 1770, beneath a large oak on the southern shore of Monterey Bay, Father Junípero Serra donned his vestments and sprinkled holy water in all directions "to rout all infernal foes." He said Mass for the members of his party, a small group of soldiers and a handful of Native Americans from Lower California who served the Crown and the Church as neophytes. Cannons were fired and bells were rung. The military commander, Captain Portola, hoisted the flag of Spain and took formal possession of the region in the name of Carlos II, King of Spain. The presidio and the mission of San Carlos Borromeo de Monterey were founded. The presidio would defend against outsiders, and the mission would win the hearts and minds of the Native Americans. The Spanish Crown could have selected no one more devoted to winning hearts and minds than Father Junípero Serra.

In zealotry, Father Serra was unsurpassed. On reaching Vera Cruz, he decided to walk to Mexico City, a distance of several hundred rugged and uphill miles. Early on the trek, he was bitten on the foot by an insect. Not only did his foot become infected, but so did his leg, yet Father Serra declined medical treatment and continued his walk. For the remainder of his life he was plagued by infections and lameness.

This incident was nothing in comparison to his other displays of devotion. He would, for example, while delivering sermons, occasionally hold aloft a crucifix while whipping himself with a chain or pounding his chest with a heavy stone. He slept on a bed of narrow wooden planks and kept nearby a whip of sharp metal studs to be used in the event that his sleep was disturbed by thoughts he judged impure. His fondest wish was to achieve martyrdom, an end which he referred to as "the real gold and silver of the Indies."

He now directed his attention to the domestication and religious conversion of the Natives of Upper California. It was his fervent wish that someday, perhaps generations hence, these people—these simple, childlike primitives as the Spanish saw them—would gain a consciousness equal to that of the Spaniards, would become *gente de razón,* people of reason, as the Spaniards considered themselves.

Within a year of the establishment of the mission at Monterey, Father Serra relocated it over the hill near the mouth of the Carmel River. There, his converts would be away from the Spanish soldiers, whose intemperate habits and immodest ways were such a bad example.

At Carmel Mission, as it came to be known, the converts were taught the fundamentals of farming and those trades which were necessary to the support of farming. Along with plowing, sewing, and harvesting, the converts learned carpentry and blacksmithing. The intention was to turn them into something equivalent to the Spanish peasantry. They would become loyal, hardworking servants of the Spanish Crown and devoted followers of the Church. When he began his efforts, Father Serra estimated that the transformation would be accomplished in about ten years. He was wrong. The transformation, in fact, would never be accomplished.

The Natives were in awe of the Spaniards' clothing and weapons, their symbols and rituals, their assertiveness and presumption of authority. They looked upon the Spaniards as mysterious, powerful beings, and out of fear and confusion, they obeyed them. For their efforts, they suffered low morale and a low birth rate, and they died by the score from disease.

By 1784, the year of his death, Father Serra had won many apparent converts, but he had also buried many. Very few Native Americans would ever become independent farmers, and none would or could return to the life they had lived for thousands of years before the arrival of the Spanish. By the end of the nineteenth century, the Natives were virtually extinct. Some of their graves are marked at Carmel Mission. Many are not. Father Serra is buried beneath the floor of the church.

Carmel Mission was, however, a grand financial success, as were other California missions. Despite the constant need to replace and train workers, the missions managed to produce large herds of cattle and excellent crops, which gave the Franciscan Fathers the greatest economic clout in all of California.

But when the Spanish Crown relinquished California to the newly independent government in Mexico City in 1822, it was discovered that the government owed the missions about five hundred thousand dollars. To eliminate this debt, the new government secularized the missions by granting mission lands to individuals to operate as private ranches. It was the end of the padres, and the beginning of the gentleman rancher—the *caballero*—and of the Yankee trader and of the American settler.

Intent upon making California economically independent, the Mexican government allowed trade with foreigners and even allowed foreigners to settle here, neither of which had been permitted under Spanish rule. Monterey was the primary port of entry, and a customs house was built. While it did not fully discourage ships from putting in at remote coves and doing business on the sly, much business was done at Monterey. American trading offices opened, and Americans began to live in Monterey. Buildings of adobe and brick began to replace the old log structures. Paths became roads which, in turn, became the streets of a town.

During the Mexican era, from 1822 to 1846, foreigners settled all over California. John Sutter built his fort and worked his fields in and around Sacramento. Americans rose to social and economic prominence in Los Angeles, San Francisco, Santa Barbara, and San Diego. Kit Carson, John Fremont, and other Americans explored the area. Wagon trains of American settlers arrived.

Though the Americans trickled in rather than poured in, their numbers began to concern the Mexican government. But before the settlement of Americans in California could evolve into much of an issue, the United States and Mexico went to war over the annexation of Texas into the Union.

With their country at war with their hosts, Americans in California decided it was a perfect opportunity to unburden themselves of the Mexican government. With the help of a small contingent of U.S. cavalry and a few ships of the U.S. Navy, the American settlers took the place. As the Native Americans had been displaced by the Spanish, and the Spanish by the Mexicans, so the Mexicans were displaced by the emigrants from the east, with one significant difference — the United States not only defeated the Mexicans in a fight for the land, they also paid for it with cash and credit. Under the terms of the Treaty of Guadalupe Hidalgo in 1848, the United States paid Mexico fifteen million dollars in cash and two million in credit against Mexican debts. These payments restored the government of Mexico to solvency. And in exchange, the United States received what is now California, Arizona, and New Mexico.

The Gold Rush of 1849 brought hundreds of thousands of people to California in the span of a few short years. But this enormous increase in population and the business and excitement it generated bypassed the Monterey Peninsula, the Carmel Valley, and the Big Sur coast. Monterey remained just a small town, a sleepy little place, important only regionally. The Carmel Valley remained pastoral; the coast and mountains of Big Sur remained wild.

Being spared the increase in population and the haphazard development that occurred elsewhere in California proved to be the salvation of the region. The natural beauty of this place has been preserved, and today it is appreciated by residents and by visitors from around the world.

■

▲ The ornateness of this restored banister in Pacific Grove is typical of Victorian architectural design. The sword fern in the background is native to coastal redwood forests.

▲ Surf rises on the shore at Pebble Beach. ▶ Inspired by the illustrations in books of fairy tales, architect Hugh Comstock designed and built numerous cottages in Carmel from the 1920s through the 1940s. This one is known as the Hansel House.

◄ Golden poppies cover hills and fields around the Monterey Peninsula from early spring through late autumn. The golden poppy is the state flower and is also the symbol of the Northern California Amateur Golf Association. ▲ One of the oldest and largest Monterey cypress in the world is the Veterans Cypress at Point Lobos. It has managed for more than a century to draw nourishment from this rocky edge of land.

▲ Sun, wind, and the ceaseless pounding of salty waves have weathered the pilings of a pier at Monterey. ▶ In the early 1900s, Cannery Row boomed with the business of canning sardines. Around 1950, when the sardines disappeared from the waters off Monterey, the canneries went out of business. These weathered, dilapidated relics are all that remain of the old canneries.

CARMEL-BY-THE-SEA

Pirates never sacked and burned Carmel-by-the-Sea, as they did Monterey. Wild-West gunslingers never dueled in the streets. Gangsters have never waged war over the lucrative ice-cream-cone and oil-painting turf of Ocean Avenue.

By the time the first cottages were built in Carmel early in the twentieth century, the pirates were long gone from the vicinity, and the Wild West had become the more or less tamed West. And if gangsters have ever been around here, they have been mighty quiet, which fits right in with the prevailing atmosphere of Carmel. Quiet is the way the residents like it, and aside from the excitements of an occasional concert in Devendorf Park, the Fourth of July fireworks over Carmel Bay, or the yearly Sand Castle Contest, deviations from tranquility are anything but encouraged and tend to be infrequent. There have certainly been incidents from time to time, and they have annoyed or amused — or a little of both — as was the case in one of the more notable incidents, the juicy sex scandal of 1926.

Known as Aimee to those who packed themselves to the rafters of her big auditorium in Los Angeles, as well as to practically everybody else, celebrated evangelist Aimee Semple McPherson had disappeared. When she reappeared about a month and a half later, she told an intricate tale about having been kidnapped and hauled off to Arizona by a couple of characters named Jake and Mexican Rose. Unfortunately for Aimee, her story was in all the newspapers, complete with photographs, and no fewer than fourteen citizens of Carmel were prepared to swear under oath that Aimee, along with the former manager of her Los Angeles radio station, had rented a cottage on Scenic Road near Ocean Avenue and stayed there together for at least a month. The hubbub went on for weeks, and for years the question most frequently posed by visitors to Carmel was, "Where's Aimee's place?"

A few years ago, Carmel went through a disturbance of the peace that made the hubbub over Aimee seem like a whisper. Clint Eastwood ran for mayor, and Carmel became media central. Reporters arrived, television remote trucks lined the streets, and hordes of the casually curious flooded the town. Everyone wanted to catch a glimpse of the famous movie star. The place was like a carnival. Residents became exasperated. Traffic jams were endless. Parking was impossible. Ultimately, Mr. Eastwood was elected, the crowds thinned out, and after serving his two-year term, he declined to run again.

In the way of incidents, Carmel's experience has been more along the lines of a certain "infamous deed," as a local newspaper called it, in which a statue of the Venus de Milo was removed in the night from a citizen's front yard and was found

---

◄ A genuine thatched roof on a stone cottage suggests the English countryside more than a town on the California coast. The unexpected in architecture is, however, common in Carmel.

the next morning positioned at the intersection of Ocean Avenue and San Antonio Street. Police got on the case and in no time they rounded up what were presumably the usual suspects, boys from local families.

Carmel is a fairly tranquil place. The reason has to do with the kind of people who live here and the kind of people who visit, which, in turn, has to do with the premise upon which Carmel was built.

At the turn of the century, a real estate man named James Franklin Devendorf, as in Devendorf Park, and a money man named Frank Powers formed the Carmel Development Company. By trading some land and paying some cash, they acquired the property that is now Carmel. They laid it out in streets and lots, and then planted pine trees all over the place. They explained their simple idea in several sentences in their promotional letter:

> . . . *California is growing so rapidly, that the time has come when the promoters of new towns can determine the general character of the residents. We want brain-workers, because they enjoy the picturesque scenery and need a climate for a vacation place so equable that they can be out-doors the whole day long.*

The *brain-workers* Devendorf and Powers sought were schoolteachers and professors, and they got them. Professors from the University of California and from Stanford University — even the president of Stanford himself, David Starr Jordan — were among those who bought lots and built cottages. The lots sold for about a hundred dollars, often on terms of five dollars down and payments of five dollars per month. If the payments were missed, Devendorf and Powers would often allow them to accumulate, without interest, sometimes for years. If it seemed certain, finally, that a buyer would never make another payment, then Devendorf and

Powers would refund every cent the buyer had already paid. At those prices and on those terms, even penniless poets could afford to buy a place in Carmel. In 1905, one such poet, George Sterling, did just that.

Mr. Sterling was an occasional and reluctant employee of a San Francisco real estate and insurance office. A man who preferred the Bohemian life of the taverns in San Francisco and aspired to the full-time turning of the poetic phrase, he came to Carmel and cut a deal.

Over the next fifteen years, Mr. Sterling drew to the fledgling town his friends and acquaintances, the artists and *literati* of the era. There were many, and among them were the authors Mary Austin, Sinclair Lewis, Jack London, and Upton Sinclair; the poet Robinson Jeffers; and the painter Xavier Martinez. Some stayed for weeks, some for months, and some for years. Mr. Jeffers stayed the rest of his life. He built *Tor House* with his own hands with stones collected from the beach, and there he resided with his family, writing his famous poetry, until his death in 1962.

Mr. Devendorf was the man who dealt directly with prospective buyers. He showed them around town, helped them choose lots, and in the process seemed to weed out the pirates, gunslingers, and gangsters. What Carmel got were residents inclined to the aesthetic, and from them came the attitude and philosophy that helped to establish a tradition of tranquility and rustic ambience, a tradition carried on today in popular sentiment and in codes and ordinances.

There have been attempts through the years to lay asphalt and erect commercial attractions at the expense of the trees, the cottages, and the beach. For the most part, these attempts have been held off. One of the citizens most instrumental in holding off the earliest attempts, and in articulating the attitude of Carmel residents toward *progress,* was Perry Newberry. He had been a news correspondent in World War I, and would later become the editor of a local newspaper. In 1926, he was a candidate for mayor. His platform, as it appeared on a placard, sums up an attitude strongly held in Carmel:

> Believing that what 9,999 towns out of 10,000 want is just what Carmel doesn't want, I am a candidate on the platform DON'T BOOST! I am making a spirited campaign to win by asking those who disagree with me to vote against me.
>
> Don't Vote for Perry Newberry
> If you hope to see Carmel become a city.
> If you want its growth boosted.
> If you desire its commercial success.
> If street lamps on its corners mean happiness to you.
> If concrete street pavements represent your civic ambitions.
> If you have less regard for the unique character of Carmel than for the opportunity of money making.
> If you think that a glass factory is of greater value than a sand dune, or a millionaire than an artist, or a mansion than a little brown cottage.
> If you truly want Carmel to become a boosting, hustling, wide-awake lively metropolis,
> DON'T VOTE FOR PERRY NEWBERRY

Perry Newberry won the election. By 1929, *progress* was deterred by the enactment of zoning laws. Only two kinds of neighborhoods would be allowed, residential and essential business, excluding a mortuary or jail.

While there are certainly more businesses here than are essential, and the roads are paved, and Carmel has enjoyed or endured — depending upon the point of view — commercial success, much of the substance and all of the spirit of Mr. Newberry's wishes have come true. There are no sidewalks or street lights in residential neighborhoods, and the houses are not numbered. Only

God can knock down a tree without appealing to the city authorities for permission to do so, and permission has been consistently hard to get. Commercial buildings and signs must conform to strict regulations of design and placement. Live music is prohibited in establishments that serve alcohol. Generally, given the restrictions that exist in Carmel, it is highly unlikely that the town will ever have a roller coaster, a Ferris wheel, a honky-tonk, a rodeo, or anything else big, loud, and flashy. It is more likely to continue to live up to the image found on a certain postcard, on which there is nothing but blackness where the picture ought to be, and the caption reads: "Carmel At Night."

Over the years, however, downtown Carmel has evolved into a kind of tourist shopping resort. People come from everywhere, and it is not surprising to walk along Ocean Avenue on any day in any season and hear any language of the world and every dialect of American. The many who wander from shop to shop usually buy something — an ice-cream cone or an oil painting or whatever it is they might be looking for or might happen upon — as if to buy something is to make the day complete. Some dine in the restaurants on hamburgers, fettucini Alfredo, baklava, what have you. Some picnic at the beach if the breeze is gentle enough.

And some linger on the sidewalk to peer into the window of an art gallery on Ocean Avenue. What holds their undivided attention is the sight of an artist at work. In a town where so many paintings are on display, the sight of one being created is rare indeed. Here, unexpectedly, is a man in a blue smock seated in front of a canvas that rests on an easel. He dabs some highlight, a bit of white, to the petal of a rose, and to the rose's reflection in a silver chalice beside it in the painting. It is an intricate piece of work, suggestive of the Italian Renaissance — an almost photographic reproduction of an actual photograph that is taped to the frame of the easel. He seems not to notice the collection of shifting faces that gaze at him through the window, faces that pause, and move on, and are replaced by new faces. This, according to the sign above the door, is the Roberto Lupetti Gallery, and this is Roberto Lupetti, the artist.

He is a man of indeterminate age, perhaps in his sixties, with wavy, light-brown hair, and a kindly manner. In the lyrical tones of an Italian accent, he says he doesn't mind at all that people watch him as he works, that he is used to it. It started, he says, by accident, when one morning the person who normally opened the gallery was unable to do so and he, Mr. Lupetti, had to open the gallery himself. He was also obliged to have a certain painting finished that day for a client. So he set up his easel in the best light, by the window, and went to work. Soon, to his surprise, a crowd was gathered on the sidewalk watching him through the window. Throughout the day, people wandered in and talked with him, and he found that he enjoyed it. Now, even though he works primarily in his studio, away from the gallery, he looks forward to coming here almost every day to spend an hour or two working on a painting, to talk with those who wander in. And, he adds with a shrug and a smile, maybe it's good for business.

Almost everybody seems to enjoy Carmel-by-the-Sea, although some might find it difficult to say exactly what it is about the place that appeals to them. They will mention the trees, the ocean, the beach, the salten air, or the shops and the restaurants. Yet there is often a sense of something else, something vague on their minds. They will dismiss it by saying, *I just like the place.*

Maybe the appeal is subliminal. Maybe it has to do with the scale upon which Carmel is built. There are no enormous steel and glass edifices here, let alone clusters of them, and there are no endless expanses of asphalt. Instead, Carmel is built on a human scale. It does not overwhelm, or intimidate, or make people feel small. It gives people an amiable sense of being in proportion, of fitting in with the surroundings rather than being dominated by them, which, according to those who study these matters, lends itself to a feeling of well-being. That might not be the only reason, but it is likely one of the reasons why so many who visit Carmel—whether they come from Kansas City, Modesto, or Yokohama—often end up saying they feel somehow at home here, that they could live in this place.

▶ After the completion of *Tor House,* Robinson Jeffers built Hawk Tower, here viewed from the beach where he collected the stones from which he constructed the tower with his own hands.

■

◄ Carmel residents would say this home is "out in the numbers," that is, outside the original one-square-mile limits of Carmel. Inside the limits, none of the homes are numbered.　▲　Never very far out of mind, the beach draws a constant stream of visitors.

▲ Where there is sunlight through the trees, there are flowers in Carmel—these in spring, when the weather has warmed and the ground is still moist from the rains.   ▶ Even a garden path in Carmel is unique. Here, a cat presides over his domain.

◄ *Misión San Carlos Borromeo del Río Carmelo,* known simply as Carmel Mission, was built by Native American labor between 1793 and 1797. The restoration of the mission in 1936 was so thorough that many consider this to be the most authentic of all the California missions. Father Junípero Serra, founder of the missions of Spanish California, is entombed beneath the floor near the altar. ▲ An autumn sun lights Carmel Mission, the mouth of the Carmel River, and Carmel Bay.

▲ An unusual dormer graces a roof in Carmel.   ▶ Architectural designs such as gates and dormers lend themselves to unique and creative treatments in Carmel. Here, no two houses, landscapes, or styles of treatment are ever the same.

◄ A dragon will light the night in a garden in Carmel. ▲ In spring, wildflowers lend color to a field in Carmel. ► ► On an autumn afternoon, cottages on a Carmel hillside bask in sunlight after the fog lifts. The view is south toward the foothills of Big Sur.

◄ A hen and chicks tell which way the wind blows in Carmel.
▲ The marshlands at the mouth of the Carmel River are protected as a refuge for ducks, pelicans, and other aquatic birds.
► ► A room at Carmel Mission is furnished in the style of the Mexican era (1822-1846). Its thick adobe walls and heavy beams are typical design and construction. This could be the *sala*—the main room—in the home of any prosperous family of the era.

▲ The early builders in Carmel gave particular attention to craftsmanship and to creating charm in the details, as seen on this garden wall. ▶ Robinson Jeffers wrote some of his poetry at this desk. His dictionary rests on the table he built of wood scavenged from the ruins of Carmel Mission.

◄ Jack Calvin—photographer, printer, journalist, and writer—built this home in 1929. John Steinbeck and Doc Rickets, both friends of Calvin, were introduced here. ▲ Carmel Point, with Carmel Beach curving northward, is where George Sterling, Jack London, and others of the literary and artistic set of early Carmel caught and cooked their abalone and held their notorious parties.

▲ This home on the beach was designed by architect Frank Lloyd Wright to resemble the bow of a ship. Completed in 1954, Mr. Wright declared it to be as "durable as rocks, transparent as a wave." ▶ A forest cottage, like many homes in Carmel, is reminiscent of the English countryside.

◄ Among the many restaurants in Carmel, Clint Eastwood's eating and drinking establishment stands in the heart of the city.
▲ The weather of Point Lobos—fog, sunshine, storm, wind, or calm—paints myriad moods, sometimes changing by the minute.

▲ Native wildflowers—California golden poppies and lupine—brighten gardens throughout the area. Working both with and against the climate, people here make their gardens a labor of love.

CARMEL VALLEY

Some years ago, a typhoon blew across an island. All that could be accomplished in the way of personal protection was to pile up mattresses and pillows at an inner corner of a little wooden house, and, behind this padding, this barricade, to curl up and ride out the storm. For more than eight hours, as seen through splintering shutters, every kind of debris—from lawn chairs to palm fronds to the occasional tree itself—flew past in a frenzy. An old Volkswagen went by at some height above the ground and at a velocity probably greater than it had ever achieved under its own power. The storm sounded like an endless barrage of hand grenades exploding against the house. It was eight hours of waiting for the roof to fly off, for some small vehicle to plow through a wall, for a coconut to crash through the shutters and spin around the room like the little ball on a roulette wheel. It was eight hours of raw fear, and it was fear unsurpassed until one moonless night under the trees on a hill above the Carmel Valley.

While sitting alone enjoying the peaceful, starry sky from a lounge on the back deck of a house, there came from the all-too-intimate nearby on the other side of the fence the scream of a mountain lion. Let no one say that levitation is impossible, not to someone who has traveled the twenty feet or so to the house, entered it, slammed the door and locked it, and done so without ever touching the back deck. Anyone could do it, anyone who hears for the first time, seemingly within arm's length, the scream of a mountain lion. The wonder of it

is this: who would have thought it could have happened practically within a golf shot of the floor of the Carmel Valley?

It seems like a civilized enough place. Drive onto the Carmel Valley Road off Highway 1 and there is a traffic light and a shopping center. In the neighborhood there are office buildings and homes, a post office, and even another shopping center. Drive a few miles farther and it becomes less urban, with orchards and pastures and crops in the fields, but there are also numerous houses, not to mention golf courses lined with condominiums. Farther on, past a winery and a few sharp bends in the road, is the Carmel Valley Village, a modest stand of restaurants, stores, gas stations, offices, a library, and a post office. The Carmel Valley Village is situated near the location of the post office, established in 1893, that first carried the name Carmel. From the village, the valley narrows and finally ends about three miles farther up the road. All in all, the valley and the hills around it are populated, settled, cut by roads, grazed on by cattle, tilled, and—in the case of golf courses—manicured. Carmel Valley can be described in many ways, but in no way can it be described as a wilderness, let alone a wilderness where mountain lions might roam.

When Robert Louis Stevenson hiked out of Monterey and passed through here in September 1879, intending to camp up in the Santa Lucia Mountains, he observed Carmel Valley and later wrote about it as "bare, dotted with chaparral, overlooked by quaint unfinished hills. The Carmel runs by many pleasant farms, a clear and shallow river, loved by wading kine."

Any kine, or cattle as they are better known today, wanting to wade in the Carmel River in September—or, for that matter, in almost any month—will be disappointed. Most of the time, there is hardly enough dampness for a kine to even moisten a hoof, let alone wade. The river has been diminished by dams, and, in more recent years, by the drilling of wells to accommodate the needs of an increasing population. This has created a river that runs only in the rainy season, in winter. In other seasons, the appearance of the river, from about the middle of the valley to the ocean, is similar to a wash in the desert that runs only in flash floods. Banks along the river have eroded. Trees have died because the water table has sunk so low. A river that used to run clear is now filled with mud and debris. What used to be a good trout stream no longer exists. The number of fish returning to spawn has decreased dramatically.

The farms referred to by Stevenson were in a way the third generation of domesticated cultivation, for the valley served first as fields and pastures for the mission. The herds of elk that the Spanish found here were eliminated because the elk competed with the mission cattle for pasture. The Spanish, who refused to eat *carne fría,* wild game, had no use for the elk.

Then came the Mexican land grants, which turned mission lands over to private owners. This began an economy exclusively dependent upon cattle hides and tallow. When California became part of the United States, land grants were broken up by sale and by marriage, and raising cattle was supplemented by raising crops and by development of other products, including Monterey Jack cheese, which was invented in Carmel Valley.

The valley had long been domesticated when the first subdivision was laid out. This was Robles del Rio, separated from what is now Carmel Valley Village by the Carmel River. In the 1920s, lots were sold, and cabins and homes were built, along with a lodge, tennis courts, a swimming pool, and a golf course winding through the hills. It was a favorite resort of movie stars such as Robert Young and Clark Gable, who enjoyed the views, the isolation, the fresh air. It was the first of several resort developments around the valley, most of them converted from farms and ranches.

The golf course at Robles del Rio, the first golf course in the valley, was, ironically, the first to succumb to drought in the late 1970s. The course is now a greenbelt and is used by hikers, joggers, and horseback riders.

Bordering the greenbelt are a few homes, some clinging to the hillsides, some resting on the flats under the elegant sprawl of oak branches. Nearby is the Ventana Wilderness, from which a variety of wild animals may wander. Deer eat roses in gardens, raccoons raid unsecured trash containers, and one summer night, shy as it is of people—probably as startled to detect a person as the person was to detect it, and probably fleeing as rapidly—came a mountain lion. The sound of its scream was chilling. And, coming as it did from the former golf course of the very first subdivision and resort around the Carmel Valley, it was a scream considerably poetic.

■

▲ During the mission era, and later in the era of Mexican land-grant ranches, the pastures of the Carmel Valley supported tens of thousands of cattle. The area continues to support cattle, as well as farms, vineyards, and—as shown here—lupine.

▲ A fallen oak lies in Robinson Canyon on Rancho San Carlos — twenty thousand acres that have been worked privately as a cattle ranch since the era of Mexican land grants. ▶ Oak and maple shade a trail in the three-thousand-acre Garland Ranch Regional Park. The miles of trails here are popular among hikers, joggers, and horseback riders. ▶ ▶ Spanish moss — also known as goat's beard — and poison oak present an elegant, colorful scene, but beware! The irritating rash from poison oak can last for weeks.

◄ A wildflower native to California, the mule ear shows a small world on a grand scale. ▲ The Carmel Valley has been horse country since the Mexican era, when gentleman ranchers took great pride in their horsemanship and in the bloodlines of their horses. Many residents today are avid riders, and some show and breed their animals professionally.

▲ In early spring, when the hills are moist from winter rains, the lupine blooms and the grass on the hills is lush and green. Though the lupine remains, the grass dies, turning the hills golden by June.   ▶ The changing hues of maple leaves bring the colors of autumn along the Carmel River.

PEBBLE BEACH

Much of what Nature created here, Samuel F. B. Morse preserved. He bought Pebble Beach and developed it, but he never called in the bulldozers to knock down the forest and make terraces of the sloping terrain, never laid out a grid of streets to build cottages from the high ground to the shore. To have done so certainly would have been less demanding of Mr. Morse's energy and imagination, possibly might have generated more profits for him, and would have conformed exactly to plans already drawn up and awaiting his approval. Pebble Beach could easily have ended up covered with pavement, traffic lights, and hamburger stands. But Mr. Morse had something else in mind.

While he was, to be sure, interested in making money, his ambition was tempered by a deep appreciation of what Nature had created here. He noticed that people were drawn to the place, that they would pay just to ride through it. His own feeling for Pebble Beach has been described as a passion. He made its preservation the primary element of his plans and the object of his continuing attention. So it is that Pebble Beach remains a dramatic, unsullied coast and a magnificent forest, much as it has been since time immemorial, and as it is meant to be, by all intentions, easements, and

---

◄ The 365-yard fourth hole at Spyglass Hill is a par four. The golf course opened in 1966, and is one of the courses that is used each year for the ATT National Pro-Am (formerly the Crosby).

regulations, forever. This is not to say that nothing has been done around here. Plenty has been done.

Pebble Beach had its modern beginnings as an excursion destination for guests of the Hotel Del Monte. In its glory days, before it was sold to the Navy in the 1940s to house the Naval Post-Graduate School, the Hotel Del Monte was a seaside resort favored by the wealthy. Guests arrived on one of the trains that traveled twice daily from San Francisco. From the station guests rode in carriages the quarter mile to "The Most Elegant Seaside Establishment in the World," as the hotel was advertised by its owner, Charles Crocker, who also owned the train, the station, Pebble Beach, and other sizable chunks of real estate in and around Monterey. When guests were not trying their hand at tennis, or selecting the suitable mashie on the Del Monte Golf Course, or strolling in the lush gardens, or taking tea on the veranda, or simply lounging on the wicker and looking ornamental, there was the excursion to Pebble Beach for a picnic and a ride by carriage—by automobile in later years—through the Del Monte Forest, down to Carmel Mission and back to the hotel along what early became known as the 17-Mile Drive. Judging by early photographs, it was all quite exhilarating, or tiresome, or—by the look of one grand dame—perturbing. Nevertheless, it became increasingly popular, and by 1909, the hotel had built an outpost at Pebble Beach.

The outpost, made of logs, was called Pebble Beach Lodge. Soon a row of rooms was added.

Known as Cottage Row, they became popular among the more robust and down-to-earth guests, those who wished to distance themselves from the strict social regimens of the hotel proper, in favor of hiking and picnicking in the forest, or collecting agates on the nearby shoreline, the *pebbled* beach, for which the greater region was named.

In 1915, Mr. Morse arrived to take charge of the hotel and its holdings. Not to be confused with his great uncle, the artist and inventor of the telegraph, Samuel Finley Breese Morse, Samuel Finley Brown Morse was faced with a big problem. The hotel was declining financially and had been for some time. Management was running the place as if it were a stuffy Victorian spa, with persnickety rules governing what guests could do, how they were expected to dress, and so forth.

Mr. Morse hired new managers, then sought ways to renew the hotel's image, to instill it with vivacity. He turned his attention to Pebble Beach. Here was potential. Among his files he found plans that would have sectioned Pebble Beach into row after row of cottages, cottages that would have destroyed the forest and the ocean views. But the question was, what could he do that would preserve the scenery and also generate income? The answer, obvious today, ingenious at the time, was golf.

In 1916, Mr. Morse hired Douglas Grant and John F. Neville, two champion amateur golfers, to design a course along the shore and cliffs. Neither of them, nor anyone else residing in the United States at the time, was a professional designer of golf courses. Yet what they designed was the Pebble Beach Golf Links, then and now one of the world's most challenging and beautiful courses.

About the time the new golf links, along with a new lodge, were dedicated in 1919, the Pacific Improvement Company informed Mr. Morse that it wanted to sell the Hotel Del Monte and all the company's holdings in and around Monterey. For Sam Morse, it was the opportunity of a lifetime.

He went to New York and borrowed a million dollars from bankers. He went to San Francisco and acquired another million from businessman Herbert Fleishhacker. He sold stock in his newly formed company for another million. Then he bought the Pacific Improvement Company for 1.3 million and was left with enough capital to operate and develop the property. Thus was born the Del Monte Properties Company, later renamed the Pebble Beach Company. Sam Morse was known as the "Duke of Del Monte," and he ran his new company and managed its lands with all the muscular regality the title implies.

Sam Morse understood that only money could preserve what was already here and create what he envisioned. He had to attract the wealthy. He lured them here to play golf, but he also had to inspire them to buy a $30,000 residential lot, then spend tens or hundreds of thousands of dollars to build a home on it. The question was, how?

The most glamorous people of the 1920s were, first, movie stars, and next, sports figures. Mr. Morse befriended Hollywood celebrities. It was no surprise on the golf links on any Saturday morning to encounter Douglas Fairbanks teeing off in the company of Mary Pickford, or Charlie Chaplin and one of his female companions saddling up at the Equestrian Center and setting off for a ride. While the movie stars were here to be seen, the leading sportsmen and sportswomen of the day were here for the more direct application of what in sales talk is called *sizzle*.

A man of wealth might arrive to play a round of golf, to spend a sporting weekend at the lodge, and find himself charmed to distraction, wined and dined in the irresistibly enchanting company of Miss So-And-So, who just last year won this and that tournament, as well as the state amateur championship. And there, too, would be Mr. You-Know-Who, whose recent triumphs on the field of play rival the performances that kept him in the headlines throughout his collegiate career.

At the opportune moment, when the brandy was being sipped and the cigars were half smoked, one of the sports figures would lean confidentially in the direction of the guest, and, as if intimating a bit of absolutely inside information, would mention that a very special, very appealing building site in the forest might be worth your seeing, as soon as possible, just between you and me.

What amiable companionship. What a wonderful place. Who could resist? It was like an invitation into an exclusive club. And, by currying wealth, that is exactly what Pebble Beach became. Sam Morse established a community of millionaires to live behind gates in the forest, in mansions overlooking the coast. By the end, the name Pebble Beach was sizzle enough.

The game of golf has been crucial to the development of Pebble Beach. Think of Paris without cafés. Think of Hong Kong without a harbor. Think, more modestly but just as critically, of Pebble Beach without golf. There would, as Miss Stein once remarked about another place, be no *there* there. Golf has been the social and economic heart of Pebble Beach, its *raison d'être,* its means of creation and continuing existence.

But there was some risk in basing the existence of Pebble Beach on the popularity of golf. In 1916, when it was decided that the Pebble Beach Golf Links would be installed, golf was not exactly America's pastime. There were, at the time, only four hundred courses in all the United States, while today there are twenty-five thousand. In the region of Monterey there was only one, the nine-hole course owned by the Hotel Del Monte.

In 1916, golf was riding the crest of a wave of enthusiasm generated by Francis Quimet. In 1913, he had defeated two great British professionals at the U.S. Open in Brookline, Massachusetts. The accomplishment made national headlines, and people took up the game in a wave of enthusiasm. Yet waves of enthusiasm, by definition, always diminish. The game could have subsided to the realm of the few in the upper echelons of society, where, before Mr. Quimet's accomplishment, golf had had its limited following. Fortunately for Sam Morse and Pebble Beach, golf came and stayed.

Bing Crosby added prestige to Pebble Beach when, in 1947, after holding his annual tournament for ten years at Rancho Santa Fe, he moved it here. It was known as the Crosby Clambake, or just the Crosby, and was the National Pro-Am Golf Championship. It was the first tournament with celebrities as the featured participants, and the first American tournament where play was carried on over more than one course simultaneously. The greatest golfers in the world were teamed with celebrities, from professional baseball and football players to musicians and movie stars. For four days in late January and early February, they braved misty wind or driving rain to play the Spyglass Hill, Cypress Point, and Pebble Beach courses. In the mid-1980s, the Crosby name was withdrawn from the tournament. The event continues as the AT&T Pebble Beach National Pro-Am Golf Championship. The proceeds still go to charity.

There are now six golf courses here: Spanish Bay, Cypress Point, Spyglass Hill, Poppy Hills, Monterey Peninsula Country Club, and Pebble Beach Golf Links. Even though ownership of the Pebble Beach Company has changed hands several times since the death of Sam Morse in 1969, his philosophy of development seems to be surviving. The six golf courses insure that almost 75 percent of the coastline remains a greenbelt.

The views and the forest remain. The 17-Mile Drive is as scenic and popular as ever. And the mansions have taken on a kind of ageless permanence, covered here by ivy, brooding there in the mist, settled on their grounds as if they were as old as the trees that surround them. And is it a wind through the branches or a ghostly whisper, *what a wonderful place . . . who could resist?*

◀ The annual Concours de'Elegance is held at Pebble Beach in August. Some of the most beautiful and rare vintage automobiles, and their elaborate hood ornaments, can be seen here. ▲ The branch of a Monterey cypress stretches over a curve on the 17-Mile Drive. For more than one hundred years, visitors have followed this route to view the spectacular forest and shore at Pebble Beach.

▲ The horsedrawn carriage is a romantic conveyance for newly-weds at Pebble Beach. Couples from around the world come here to be married. ▶ The Crocker Cypress Grove at Cypress Point was set aside as a natural reserve in 1952.

◄ The life cycle of Monterey cypress is played out on the rocky shore. One of Pebble Beach's earliest mansions can be glimpsed in the distance between the living trees. ▲ An unexpected gust of wind can send the ball into the ocean at the seventh hole of the Pebble Beach Golf Links. ► ► The sixteenth hole at Cypress Point Golf Course requires a drive off the tee over water, which makes it one of the most challenging holes in the world.

▲ The sea comes up as a winter storm approaches. Soon the water will darken to the deepest gray, and foam will cover the rocks.
► A tranquil harbor, Stillwater Cove deserves its name.

PACIFIC GROVE

Set as it is between the glittering spectacle of Cannery Row and the dramatic beauty of Pebble Beach, Pacific Grove is refreshingly unglittering and undramatic.

This town is like a middle sister, less pretty perhaps, less bubbly to be sure, accustomed to being sometimes overlooked. But this doesn't seem to bother her. She is not the type to fuss or carry on about herself. She is too busy, and would find it curious, maybe a bit suspicious, maybe slightly annoying, if others showed her any great fawning attentiveness. She goes about her business quietly, unassumingly, without pretense or apology. There is a down-to-earth substance about her, a modesty and lightheartedness that makes her entirely comfortable to be with.

Take a walk along Lighthouse Avenue and here will be citizens out buying a rubber washer for the faucet; picking up tax forms from the preparer; browsing in the second-hand record, tape, and CD shop; or making a purchase at a bookstore. Everywhere, people are going about their business, riding bicycles, jogging, walking their dogs. Around Pebble Beach, the attire is often golf togs or jodhpurs. Around Carmel, there are lots of bulky sweaters and Greek fisherman's caps. But along Lighthouse Avenue, denims, jogging outfits, or bicycle togs prevail. Comfort seems to have the edge over style and beauty.

◄ Sunset, such as this one viewed from Pacific Grove, may truly epitomize a "sailor's delight."

Now, turn down a side street and here, without neon or fanfare, is a café, clean and bright, with big front windows. It has a neighborhood feel about it. First names are tossed around between the owner, who is a man with a Latin accent, and the clientele. The clientele are pure Pacific Grove, youngish and casual. Yet there is a Greek fisherman's cap on the premises, worn by a bearded man in a bulky sweater. And there is even a pair of jodhpurs, worn by a lady dragging one long, manicured fingernail in tight circles on the blue-checkered tablecloth. Her companion, a woman in a pricey-looking dress, seems to be conveying a serious cosmic secret. Everyone else is sipping beers and digging into tamales. It seems they came here to eat, not to see or be seen. And the feeling is conveyed that this is also true—at least the part about not wanting to see or be seen—for the jodhpur lady and her companion.

Now, take a ride up the hill into a residential neighborhood. Here are kids playing baseball at the school field. In a driveway, a man is working under the hood of his car. Down the block stands a child's swing set, the empty seat still swinging. Here is a ranch house; there, a Victorian. And there is a row of little wooden houses, narrow abodes set so close together that a person could barely squeeze between them.

In front of one of these, in a postage-stamp of a front yard, stands a large woman looking as sturdy as an old stove. Wearing a flowered, billowy dress and a big sun hat with wisps of gray and reddish hair poking below the brim, she is clipping her roses, and, by the look on her face—by the furrowed brow, by the set of her jowly jaw, and by the quick snip, snip of the clippers—she definitely means business. It is easy to imagine that the kids in her neighborhood, the ones playing baseball up at the school, go out of their way to pass her house on the opposite side of the street. She looks the type who would not hesitate to give them the full force of a piece of her mind. Come to think of it, let's move on.

What is here in Pacific Grove is a slice of life, young and old, foreign and domestic. People here own the cafés and the tax service. They caddie at Pebble Beach, or run a shop in Carmel, or they are retired and play mahjong until Vanna comes on at seven. They own homes, raise children, cut their lawns on Saturday morning, and go to church on Sunday. That, at least, is the impression Pacific Grove gives. These are regular, good old American folks, by the look and feel of the place. But where is the grove? Where is the cluster of trees one expects to find around here?

Pacific Grove was once exactly that, a place covered with trees. Around 1875, when a religious group built a retreat, the trees began to fall.

It seems a minister decided that this forest near the sea would be an excellent place for inspiring the sinful and leading them to repentance. In the summer, the faithful arrived and erected tents, between the trees, and twice daily they sought inspiration at camp meetings. The way to Heaven from this Piney Paradise was marked by strict rules. There could be no tobacco, liquor, late hours, dancing, card-playing, or loud talking. It might sound as if it were a dreadful place, not so much because of what was prohibited, but because of the people who busied themselves making sure the prohibitions were observed. But Pacific Grove was, believe it or not, a popular retreat. And soon the forest began to fall. Tents snugged between trees gave way to cabins. Trees were felled in clusters to make room for larger cabins, followed by houses, roads, and stores.

At first, people lived here only in summer. In 1879, Robert Louis Stevenson happened upon the place in the off-season and recorded his impressions as follows:

> One day—I shall never forget it—I had taken a trail that was new to me. After a while the woods began to open, the sea to sound nearer at hand. I came upon a road. . . . A step or two further, and without leaving the woods, I found myself among trim houses. I walked through street after street. . . . The houses were all tightly shuttered; there was no smoke, no sound but of waves, no moving thing. I have never been in a place that seemed so dream-like. . . . This town had plainly not been built above a year or two, and perhaps had been deserted overnight. Indeed it was not so much like a deserted town as like a scene upon the stage by daylight, and with no one upon the boards. The barking of a dog led me at last to the only house still occupied, where a Scotch pastor and his wife pass the winter alone in this empty theater. The place was "The Pacific Camp Ground, the Christian Seaside Resort."

Pacific Grove was a curiosity to Stevenson, and possibly a nightmare to the devil, but it was too much the fanatic's dream to continue very long as it was. The property's owners, the managers of the Pacific Improvement Company, a cigar-smoking, bottom-line crowd if ever there was one, sold lots to anybody who wanted to buy. Some buyers, while they might have been Christians, were not the kind of Christians that the potentates of the Piney Paradise wished to embrace and call their own. No sir, these were tobacco-smoking, snuff-dipping, liquor-swilling, loud-talking, naked-in-the-moonlight-swimming, card-playing, late-night, carrying-on-something-fierce Christians. They were irredeemably backslid, the type to show up for services on Sunday morning with a hangover and a new tattoo. Soon, Pacific Grove faded as a religious retreat, and the town grew.

The grove was so thoughtlessly done away with that its passing could be considered practically accidental. It was not that someone was intent on knocking down trees. It was rather that they were intent on building a town, and the trees went down as the town went up. Today, Pacific Grove might just as well be called, Pacific, period.

Then again, there is Asilomar, heavily forested and considered by many to be a part of Pacific Grove, although it actually is a state park that adjoins Pacific Grove. Asilomar, meaning "refuge by the sea," is from the Latin *asylum,* "refuge," and *mare,* "sea." It began in 1913 as a retreat for the Young Women's Christian Association. In 1956, the state received the property, some of it by sale and some of it by donation, from the YWCA. Its affairs were administered by the Pacific Grove city government until 1969, when the state took over those duties. It is used as a retreat and conference center by business and professional people.

One of the most mysterious and enchanting aspects of Pacific Grove is the monarch butterfly. The butterflies spend the winter here, and have every winter for as long as anyone can remember. They arrive in late October, early November at the latest, and they cover the trees in the George Washington Park and the Monterey pines near the Butterfly Grove Inn. The monarchs are to look at rather than to touch, for to molest them in any way brings a fine of five hundred dollars, and time in jail, too, if the molestation seems particularly obnoxious. The monarch is so highly regarded here that a statue in its honor has been erected in Lovers Point Park. The Chamber of Commerce brochures often refer to Pacific Grove as "The Butterfly Capital of the World." And in 1991, the Monterey County Board of Supervisors declared the monarch butterfly to be the county's official insect. The word around here is, don't show up with a net.

No one understands all the reasons why the butterflies spend the winter here, though it is certain that the climate—the microclimate, to put a finer edge to it—is precisely correct for the survival of the species at a certain point in their lives. Microclimate has to do with temperature, humidity, wind, and the kind of vegetation and the amount of oxygen and carbon dioxide in a particular vicinity. The climatic balance required for the survival of the monarch is delicate. Although monarchs do not hibernate, they do slow down in winter and live off the fat built up in their bodies. If the temperature is too warm, they use up too much energy and perish before spring, when it is time for them to mate. To disturb their habitat could mean the end of the monarch around here.

The people of Pacific Grove are determined to protect the butterflies, to continue to have their trees covered with the brilliant orange and black, to have the monarchs fluttering around town from October to March. And they honor the butterfly with a parade every year, in which a couple of thousand school children dress up as monarchs and march around town. People come from all around to attend the festivities, which include not only the parade, but also a carnival and bazaar.

Who is that winding through the crowd, carrying a little boy—a grandchild perhaps—and gently dabbing at his nose with a tissue? That sun hat, those gray and reddish wisps, aren't they familiar?

■

▲ Window panes of pressed glass were common in the Victorian era. Such details of design are preserved in many of the older homes in Pacific Grove. ▶ A door of a Victorian in Pacific Grove shows how color is used to enhance the ornate woodwork.

◄ An excellent example of a beautifully restored Pacific Grove
Victorian home, this one now serves as a restaurant. ▲ Surf
pounds the coast endlessly—shifting sands, smoothing rocks, and
providing an ever-changing view for contemplation.

▲ The Point Piños Lighthouse, completed in 1854, is the oldest lighthouse in continuous operation on the West Coast. There is no longer a lighthouse keeper, however, for the operation of the light is now automatic. The lower section is a museum containing maritime artifacts. ▶ The sun sets at Pacific Grove.

◄ The Gosby House, an inn built in 1887, still operates today. Here, a member of the staff reclines on the front porch. ▲ The early twentieth-century architecture of Pacific Grove dates from the period when the tents and cabins of religious retreats gave way to more permanent structures.

▲ Patterns in the glass show through the lace curtains of a Pacific Grove Victorian. ▶ Stained glass and statuary are reminiscent of the early years in Pacific Grove.

◄ Once a private residence, this meticulously restored Victorian now serves as a popular bed-and-breakfast—The Seven Gables. Its furnishings are virtual museum pieces, from glass, to tables, to chandeliers. It stands on Ocean View across from Lover's Point.   ▲ A mountain lion, forever vigilant in stone, guards a wall near 6th and Lighthouse in Pacific Grove.

▲ Whales appear not only on ornately-peaked rooftops in Pacific Grove but also offshore during their twice-yearly migrations.
▶ A beautiful example of one of Pacific Grove's small Victorian cottages dating back nearly to the turn of the century.

BIG SUR

When the Spanish explorers marched northward from San Diego they traveled near the coast, until they reached a point north of what is now San Simeon, where they stopped and decided there was no way they were going to subject themselves and their animals to these rugged, foreboding mountains. The mountains were practically vertical from the ocean up to the clouds — and they were not low clouds, either. So the Spanish turned around and went south a few miles, then inland, then north again, finally reaching Monterey by a route still used by travelers more interested in speed and comfort than in highway adventure.

Those who choose the coastal route enter the mysterious mountains of *Big Sur. El País Grande del Sur,* the big country to the south, is a land where mountain lions live, where sea lions sunbathe on the beaches, where the redwoods are magnificent, where to sip a refreshing beverage on the deck of a restaurant high on a mountainside overlooking the great expanse is a genuine, relaxing, soul-soothing pleasure.

But, to clarify a point: The name *Big Sur* is not particularly specific. Big Sur can refer to the coast and the mountains from just south of Point Lobos to just north of San Simeon. That covers a lot of territory. Or, it can refer exclusively to a community on Highway 1, where the state has

erected signs about two miles apart. The signs inform drivers from each direction that they are entering Big Sur. Many feel this reference is too limited. Some say Big Sur refers only to an area near the Big Sur River; others say the name refers to something else. For the sake of discussion here, Big Sur will refer to the coast and mountains from Point Lobos in the north to San Simeon in the south.

It is quite a drive from Monterey. Highway 1 narrows and twists. There are places where the cliffs go off into the deep dark nowhere. On particularly foggy nights, the driver may see his life pass before him in an instant as he hunts for the white line on the road and tries to stick to it.

On a clear day, the views from this curving band of often precariously elevated asphalt are breathtaking. The views are immense; Big Sur deserves its name. Here are the big green-and-golden mountains, and there is the big blue sky and the big blue sea. There might be a ship ten miles out, giving the impression of a child's toy on a pond. Cities somehow cease to exist, or to be important, or to have much relevance to any truly satisfying possibilities. Big Sur can do that, can make so much seem so petty by comparison. This place is another world. It is not a place where perspective is gained. It is a place where perspective is imposed irresistibly, almost with a whack.

The components of modern American civilization, such as shopping malls and tracts of split-level houses, do not exist around here. Actual

---

◄ Rising almost vertically from the ocean, these mountains forced the Spaniards inland as they trekked northward from San Diego to Monterey.

residents, the hardy breed of bona fide, year-round dwellers who occupy houses and cabins along the dirt roads up the canyons and on the mountainsides, are estimated to number in the hundreds rather than the thousands. Living here can be the definition of the word *isolated.* Those who have chosen to live here are a mixed group: ranchers descended from ranchers, working the land for a modest living; people employed at the few businesses and resorts; and a number of naturalists, artists, and retirees—even a Nobel Prize winner.

Probably the most famous resident, to some the most controversial, and one who emboldened the print of Big Sur on the map, was Henry Miller. Many around the world have read his book, *Big Sur and the Oranges of Hieronymus Bosch.* Mr. Miller loved the isolation. "Artists," he once remarked, "don't live in colonies. Ants do."

Lawrence Ferlinghetti, poet and owner of the City Lights bookstore in San Francisco, owned a cabin at Bixby Creek, and there Jack Kerouac spent a summer drinking himself into oblivion and also managing somehow to compose his novel, *Big Sur.*

Big Sur's reputation as a place where the unconventional experimented with altered consciousness was probably advanced by the establishment of the Esalen Institute. Here, about forty miles south of Carmel, situated between Highway 1 and the ocean, is the site of what was once the Big Sur Hot Springs.

On weekends in the late summer and autumn of 1962, the owners of the hot springs sponsored a series of seminars on "Human Potentiality." The program grew into the Esalen Institute, described in its literature as a place to explore "those trends in education, religion, philosophy, and the physical and behavioral sciences which emphasize the potentialities and values of human existence." *Time* magazine referred to Esalen as an "Aquarian think tank," but there is considerably more to it than that glib description suggests. Alan Watts, who studied the major cultures and religions of the world and wrote volumes about them, delivered numerous lectures at Esalen. Here, too, an obscure Harvard professor, Dr. Timothy Leary, held seminars on a new, mind-altering substance, LSD, and suggested that people "turn on, tune in, and drop out."

What goes on around here more than anything else these days is hiking. Perhaps the best-known, most accessible place for it is Pfeiffer Big Sur State Park, off Highway 1 about twenty-eight miles south of Carmel. Its trails winding through a redwood forest, Pfeiffer lies in the lower valley of the Big Sur River. The park—with a lodge, cabins, a restaurant, and about two hundred campsites—has been here since 1933. The redwoods, many of them, have been here for hundreds of years. And among them live all kinds of wildlife.

Big Sur borders Ventana Wilderness Preserve, which lies to the east. All animals of the region, from quail to deer to bobcats, from squirrels to snakes to banana slugs, are protected here. While some people have seen the tracks of mountain lions, few have seen the lions themselves. Nonetheless, it is wise to keep pets from wandering at night. Mountain lions, as well as other predators in the area, tend to be all business, and family pets are no match for them.

Big Sur is a wild and rugged place, remote and sparsely populated. Owing to restrictions on development and the difficulty of the terrain, it is likely to remain so. To have it any other way would be a loss not only to the wildlife and the environment, but also to the best parts of the human spirit.

■

▲ Highway 1 rolls and curves with the sloping terrain of Big Sur. Mudslides in winter and heavy fog in summer can make this stretch of road between Carmel and San Simeon one of the most challenging routes in California.

▲ This autumn storm will turn the golden hillside lush and green. So it will remain until the rains cease in late spring. ▶ Young redwood trees thrive in the canyons of Big Sur. This is a typical redwood forest, with ferns, clover, and the occasional Douglas fir. The scent is musty, and the air is often damp.

◄ The limb of an oak tree stands out against the dense fog on a morning in Big Sur. Oaks range widely throughout California.
▲ A sycamore leaf floats toward the ocean on the Big Sur River.

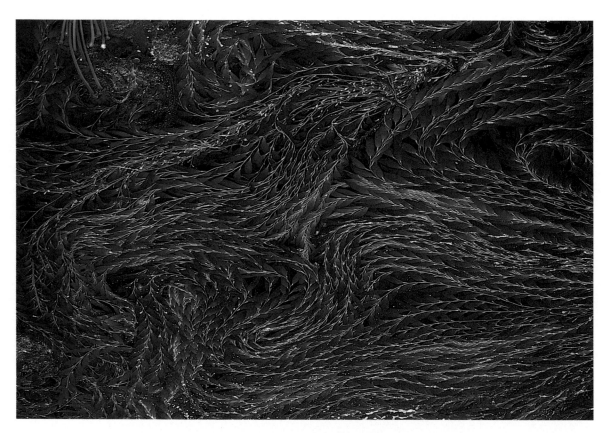

▲ Kelp, food to a variety of sea life, grows eight to ten inches per day. Among its other uses, kelp is an ingredient for soap and nutritional products. ▶ Trees and foliage grow thickly along the Big Sur River. ▶ ▶ Fog shrouds the horizon on a summer day.

◄ The views in Big Sur are frequently softened by the fog.
▲ A blanket of fog extends above the ocean all the way to the horizon, a classical view during summer in Big Sur.

▲ Wind, rain, and runoff have curiously eroded this cliff into row after row of cones. ▶ The original coast highway, unpaved and impassable without a four-wheel-drive vehicle in winter, serves as main street to some residents of Big Sur.

◄ Thick growth and the struggle for light twist limbs and trunks in a Big Sur canyon. ▲ Molera Ranch, established in the nineteenth century, has been part of the 4,786-acre Andrew Molera State Park since 1972. In the park are bridle trails, picnic areas, camp sites, and one of the finest beaches in all of Big Sur.

▲ Oaks, madrones, and redwoods thrive in protected canyons between the arid slopes of Big Sur. ▶ The Big Sur coast is rugged, much of it inaccessible to all but sea lions and sea otters, who find here an excellent habitat.

MONTEREY

On November 23, 1818, Monterey was sent a message, an ultimatum that put the residents in a panic. It read as follows:

Dear Sir: Since the King of Spain has declared bloody war on the Americans who do not wish to exist under his dominion, these same Americans have to make a defense by waging war on land and sea. They make war with all the seriousness of purpose and with all the right of nations. Therefore, having crossed the Pacific Ocean to this coast, I now desire the surrender of your city with all the furniture and other belongings of the King. If you do not do so, the city will be reduced to cinders, and also the other surrounding villages. It is within my power to bring about this destruction. You may evade all the above spilling of blood by agreeing to my proposal. If so, I shall desist from what I say. Be good enough to reply to me as soon as possible. May God keep you many years.

Hippolyte de Bouchard

Earlier in the day, two ships had sailed into view around Point Piños. The smaller ship sailed close to the shore and, upon reaching the waters in front of the presidio, dropped anchor and opened fire. The forty soldiers garrisoned at the presidio set up a battery on the beach and sent back a brisk fire of cannon balls that tore into the attacking ship. Then the other ship approached and, under a flag of truce, sent the ultimatum.

The governor's reply was a note dripping with defiance and indignation. Captain Bouchard must have welcomed this, for he seems to have been the kind of sea captain who was always just itching for a fight.

At some point in his recent career, he alleged legitimacy through an affiliation with something called the Republic of Buenos Aires. Lately, his ship, the *Argentina,* and its smaller, trigger-happy companion, the *Santa Rosa,* had been sacking and burning the coasts of New Spain. Just now, Captain Bouchard was on a return cruise from Hawaii where he had made some quick cash by selling off some gold chalices and silver crucifixes. At Monterey he hoped to fill his holds again.

About the time the governor's reply was being rowed out to Captain Bouchard, the governor grabbed his keepsakes and headed for parts more peaceful, in the general direction of what is now Salinas. Monterey's residents, noticing that the only sign of their governor was a wake of dust leading out of town, themselves went into somewhat of a frenzy of keepsake gathering and of heading rapidly inland.

The next morning, when Captain Bouchard landed, he was accompanied by three hundred fifty cutthroats from Spain, England, France, Portugal, Australia, and the Pacific Islands. Some of the pirates had not even bothered to dress for the

---

◄ Fishing boats, charter boats, and pleasure craft share Monterey's harbor in light fog at sunrise.

115

occasion. They came overboard buck naked and returned splendiferous in the attire of Spanish colonial dandies.

It took them about four days to pillage and burn the town and presidio, and tear up the orchards and gardens. Only blackened, smoldering ruins were left. Instead of letting loose a volley of cannon balls, Captain Bouchard might simply have sent a note expressing an interest in spending a night of dancing the fandango and the *jarabe tapatío* or of witnessing a bear and bull fight, and his reception would almost certainly have been warmer. The people of Monterey knew how to treat visitors, knew how to make them feel welcome. As a matter of fact, the people of Monterey were often downright desperate to have visitors.

Monterey was an isolated outpost, a half-forgotten extremity of a half-forgotten territory of a fading empire. News from the outside world came only by infrequent visits from Spanish ships or by word-of-mouth along the mission trail. Stale news it always was, its accuracy often distorted. Of equal importance to the news was the chance to get pots and pans, a bolt of cloth, and other household necessities and luxuries. The authorities of the Spanish Empire expected the people of Monterey to rely for their needs solely upon Spanish ships, and the authorities took a very dim view of any visits by foreigners. It was their position that the whole point of Monterey's existence was to keep foreigners away from California, to hold up a big sign, "OCUPADO, DO NOT DISTURB." Yet no prohibitions could alter the fact that whenever a mast broke the horizon, spirits in Monterey lifted and preparations for barbecues began. If it were the mast of a foreign vessel, the local authorities tended to turn their heads, the foreigners were welcomed, and the party was on.

Between 1822 and 1846, the Mexican era, prohibitions against foreigners were lifted. Foreigners were encouraged to visit, even to settle here as residents, the idea being that foreigners would bring trade, and trade would bring economic self-sufficiency to California, a primary goal of the Mexican government. And it worked. Foreigners did bring trade, and trade did bring prosperity, and the people of Monterey settled into a pleasant, fairly easy life.

What they traded were cattle hides and tallow, produced on the ranches created from the lands formerly owned by the missions. These ranches produced a new class of individual, the gentleman rancher, the *caballero,* an expert horseman, but otherwise a man of leisure. He was a kind of showpiece, garbed exquisitely, with special emphasis on silver buckles and spurs and accessories on his handcrafted saddle. This was, of course, his party outfit, worn to the frequent celebrations and entertainments: the horse races, the dances, the bear and bull fights. The caballero was a dashing, courtly figure, romantic and carefree. He personified the tone, the attitudes, and the aspirations of his society. His loyalties were to his family, his property, and his community. He was born here and he thought of himself not so much as a Spaniard or a Mexican, but as a *Montereño* or a *Californeo.*

Unfortunately for the caballero, the complexities of the world intruded upon him and rendered him obsolete. It happened quickly. On July 7, 1846, Commodore Sloat raised the U.S. flag over the Customs House and the United States acquired all of California. As Senator Hayakawa once put it, "We stole it fair and square," when the caballero was, it seems, catching up on his sleep.

Soon Monterey was no longer the capital of California. The Gold Rush made San Francisco the prominent port city. Sacramento boomed as well. And Monterey became an even sleepier little town. By the first week of September in 1879, when Robert Louis Stevenson found his way here, Monterey, with its white adobes and red tile roofs, appeared to be the same modest little Mexican town it had been in the 1840s.

Robert Louis Stevenson was in love with Fanny Osbourne, an American divorcée he had met in France. Although he was penniless, he managed to raise enough money to sail in steerage to New York, then ride the train across the continent to follow Fanny Osbourne to Monterey. It was a difficult journey, practically a trip to the end of the earth in those days, and it lasted nearly one month. Mr. Stevenson's health, bad from the beginning, worsened along the way. Yet, he later claimed, he never thought of turning back. The man who would write *Treasure Island* and *Kidnapped* was determined to marry Mrs. Osbourne.

Some claim he lived at a house known today as Stevenson House, at 510 Houston Street, though there is some dispute about that. Others claim he lived in a house, now torn down, adjoining the former residence of Thomas Larkin. Wherever it was that he actually lived, Mr. Stevenson enjoyed Monterey. He wrote to a friend that it was "a lovely place, which I am growing to love."

Here, he took up a routine. Aside from his writing and his visits with Mrs. Osbourne, he checked the post office for his mail, picked up a newspaper at an establishment called Handsell's, then installed himself for a midday meal—his only meal of the day—at the restaurant of Jules Simoneau. As he wrote in a letter, he sat "in Simoneau's little whitewashed back-room, round a dirty tablecloth with François the baker, perhaps an Italian fisherman, perhaps Augustin Dutra, and Simoneau himself."

Mr. Stevenson was frequently ill and always short of cash. But then the editor of the local newspaper hired him as a part-time reporter at a salary of two dollars per week. This went a long way toward helping Mr. Stevenson, and he never did learn that the editor could not afford to hire him at any wage, that it was Mr. Simoneau and his friends who provided the money to pay his salary.

Hiking was one of his favorite pastimes, and he hiked all around the Monterey Peninsula, Point Lobos, through the Carmel Valley, and into the Santa Lucia Mountains. It is a popular belief and a scholarly supposition that areas of Pebble Beach and Point Lobos were the inspiration for settings in his novel, *Treasure Island*. Mr. Stevenson did marry Fanny Osbourne, and they lived happily until his death in Samoa in 1894.

John Steinbeck, the other writer so famously associated with Monterey and Monterey County, was in his day not especially popular among the business community and the socially prominent of Salinas and Monterey. The problem with John Steinbeck, in the view of his local critics, was that he wrote stories about drunkards, finagling *paisanos,* and other unsavory types, and, in the end, the unsavory types emerged as more noble, true, and generally more virtuous than the solid citizenry depicted in his stories. *Tortilla Flat* and *The Long Valley* particularly riled the local critics. In these books there were characters based on prominent local personalities, veiled but thinly. The author was, in the opinion of his local critics, an unmitigated degenerate.

It is amazing, though, what a Pulitzer Prize and a Nobel Prize can do in the way of rehabilitating an unmitigated degenerate. Today in Salinas, the former hotbed of Steinbeck bashing, a brick tossed in almost any direction, from almost any spot in town, is likely to land on something named in his honor. The most obvious reminder of Mr. Steinbeck in Monterey is Cannery Row. Here is the setting for his novel of the same name, published in 1945.

In Mr. Steinbeck's day, Cannery Row, then known as Ocean View Avenue, was booming with sardine canneries. From about 1900 to about 1950, before the sardines mysteriously disappeared from the waters off Monterey, Cannery Row was almost one full mile of noisy, smelly, gritty industrialization, often going full blast twenty-four hours a day. The sidewalks were slick with who-knew-what; the bay was slick with a layer of diesel fuel.

The kind of people who now inhabit the place are not the kind of people who then inhabited the place, nor are the businesses remotely similar. It was a rough neighborhood, with noisy little honky-tonks and dingy little flophouses, with the occasional inebriate winding down the street, with a knife fight now and then, with ladies of easy virtue loitering around the lamp posts. About Cannery Row, in his novel, Mr. Steinbeck wrote this:

Cannery Row is the gathered and scattered tin and iron and rust and splintered wood, chipped pavement and weedy lots and junk heaps, sardine canneries of corrugated iron, honky tonks, restaurants and whore houses, and little crowded groceries and flophouses.

Not anymore. Today the canneries are gone, torn down, burned down, or rebuilt into retail establishments and restaurants. The area has been reformed, shined up, repainted, given new sidewalks and has become a place of its own. The old inhabitants are long gone, replaced by ubiquitous teenagers, older folks with grandchildren toddling along beside them, tourists foreign and domestic, out to buy a T-shirt or taste some wine or sit down to eat a club sandwich.

The true prize of Cannery Row today is the Monterey Bay Aquarium, a huge structure located at the far end of Cannery Row, almost in Pacific Grove. In it, waiting to be seen and learned about, are some five thousand animals, amounting to about three hundred species, all beautifully exhibited in approximately twenty habitational galleries. Looking through its windows at the reef over here, at the octopus over there, summons a question: what is most worth preserving? Then gazing through a window at a pair of spectacularly colorful fish, with children and parents bumping around to get a better view, narrows the question to this: is a sardine processing plant,

one that for years rumbled and reeked on this very site, more important, more appealing, more educational, more healthy, more worthy of visiting, and generally more valuable than this fine aquarium? Probably, very probably, no.

In other parts of town, little has changed in a hundred or more years. Many of the streets run the same courscs, and there are about forty buildings that were erected a century and a half ago. These buildings are the famous adobes, made from the clay that covers the hills around here. They have been restored and freshened up with gardens and tile courtyards, and many of them continue to serve as homes and offices, public and private. These handsome old buildings are a suggestion of what is important to Monterey. As with Cannery Row, the past is used to create an attractive ambience in the present.

Monterey is a financial center for the agricultural economy of the county, as it has been for much of its history. It is also a working port from which fishing vessels operate. The military at the presidio, at the Naval Post-Graduate School, and at Fort Ord contribute to its economic well-being. Yet these endeavors and institutions are insufficient to support the city completely.

For a while after the sardines were gone and the canneries went out of business, the city had to figure out what to do to make up for the lost jobs and revenue. The answer was all around Monterey, in its old buildings, in the beauty of its setting, in its history. What was here would become the foundation of the city's primary business: the business of hospitality — conventions and tourism. Directly and indirectly, hospitality and its supporting enterprises account for about half of all the employment in Monterey.

As a result, industry of any kind that might in any way pollute the environment is banned. The sardine canneries could not return even if the sardines did. The waterfront and the bay are clean and picturesque, and can be an excellent place to observe otters and seals, and to watch the lumbering pelicans as they dive for their dinners like great crashing kites.

Monterey is far enough removed from the routinely beaten path that most people who come here do so by intention rather than by accident. It is near enough the major cities to serve for many as a weekend retreat.

These aspects of the place were confirmed late one evening in a restaurant overlooking the bay. Only two couples still occupied tables, the tables fairly close together. While one couple was sipping their coffee and the last of their wine, the other couple lingered over their salmon and champagne, chatting softly and gazing out the window at the lights bobbing around the pier. In one of those unavoidable meetings of glances, in the camaraderie of sharing a small section of a large room, remarks were called for and made. "I suppose we're keeping the place open," said the man who was still eating. "Why don't you help us finish the champagne?"

The other couple smiled and replied that they couldn't possibly.

Please, said the man, he and his wife couldn't finish it. As the other couple relented, the man lifted the bottle out of the bucket and drained it into their glasses. Remarks then fell into that easier rhythm that can pass among strangers who feel it might be pleasant to talk with one another.

The couple sharing their champagne had come down for the weekend. The last of their children to be married had done so earlier in the month.

That would be good reason to celebrate, the other couple remarked.

Well, it was a little more than that, replied the man. Then he and his wife smiled to themselves, and exchanged an almost imperceptibly quick glance that made an almost tangible connection between them, carrying with it an understanding, an acknowledgment, as if they were communicating by means greater than a glance, means that could register thoughts, feelings, heartbeats. There was about it an intimacy and a mature lightheartedness, a suggestion of two dear old friends who had depended on each other, who had seen the ups and downs, the good and bad, and had seen it through together.

Soon, with the champagne gone, the thank-yous given, and the good-byes exchanged, there came the walk outside into the chilly summer night, and the full realization that love had been witnessed—tried and true, the genuine article. This realization somehow made the air cooler, made the lights around the bay brighter, made the boats bobbing and swaying on the shadowy water even more picturesque. And with this scenery in view, possibly etched forever as a snapshot in the memory, there came another indelible impression, that this place was made for people like that.

■

◄ On a wall at the José Castro adobe, known as *La Mirada,* French tiles depict Continental scenes. ▲ Stevenson House is said to have been Robert Louis Stevenson's residence when he visited Monterey in 1879. This old adobe was operated as the French Hotel—a spartan establishment patronized primarily by sailors.

▲ For a time in the 1840s, this building was the quarters of a young lieutenant in the United States Army, William Tecumseh Sherman. Around Sherman's time, it also served as lodging for John C. Fremont. Now the plaster has chipped and fallen away, exposing the original adobe bricks. ▶ This heavy door, with its ornate metal work, is in the Spanish tradition.

◄ At Monterey Bay Aquarium, kelp grows in this three-story-high exhibit—the tallest indoor aquarium exhibit in the world. Made of acrylic strong enough to hold back over three hundred thousand gallons of water, the windows are more than seven inches thick. This tank holds leopard shark, sardines, and other sea life native to the region.　▲ The colors of sunset are reflected between the angled pilings at Monterey Bay.

▲ Boats crowd Monterey Harbor. ▶ Monterey Bay Aquarium, with more than five thousand animals of more than three hundred species, opened in 1984. It occupies the site on Cannery Row where the Hovden Cannery once stood. In the foreground are the shacks, built in the 1920s, where the early cannery workers lived.

◄ Edward F. Rickets, marine biologist and co-author with John Steinbeck of the *Sea of Cortez,* was the model for the character of Doc in the novel *Cannery Row.* This building on Cannery Row once housed the Pacific Biological Laboratories, owned and operated by Mr. Rickets. ▲ Soon after sunrise, fishing boats anchored in Monterey Bay will head into the fog bank in the distance.

▲ Once hunted nearly to extinction, sea otters now occupy coastal waters from southern Big Sur to northern Monterey Bay. Otters are playful creatures, delightful to watch.

POINT LOBOS

A walk around here at sunrise on a summer day can be an eye-opener, can get the heart going. The air is calm but chilly, with fog hovering around the trees. The only sound is an occasional muffled splash from the ocean, washing against some distant rock, or perhaps closer, just below the cliff. Distances are difficult to gauge. Views are limited. Noises are magnified, or are they muffled? That terrific thrashing in the brush just now, was it far off and is whatever made it fleeing or approaching? Now, with the heart beating more rapidly, the question becomes this: what is a sensible human being who is not exactly ranger material doing around here at this time of day, anyhow?

It is difficult to imagine that Point Lobos, 2.5 miles south of Carmel, was once the site of various domestic enterprises. It has served at different times as the location of a farm, a whaling station, a Chinese fishing village, a depot from which the coal mined out of the local hills was loaded onto ships, and as a bootleggers' delivery point. Today, it is the Point Lobos State Reserve, a park encompassing 1325 acres, 775 of them under water. Among other things, this means that no one is supposed to come here and pry abalone off the rocks, cast a line into the sea, or dig for mussels. This is a place to watch the birds dive for fish, and the seals and sea lions sun themselves, or, in the right season, to catch a glimpse of whales. It is also one of the only two places on earth — the other being Pebble Beach — that is the native habitat of the Monterey cypress *(Cupressus macrocarpa).*

The grove on the northern shore of Point Lobos seems to grow out of the granite. The ancestry of these trees can be traced ten thousand years, back to when the climate was cooler, when glaciers were carving up much of California. It is believed that cypress forests ranged up and down the central coast. But as the climate warmed, the trees died out. They have survived, however, at Pebble Beach and here at Point Lobos because of cool temperatures and high humidity. These are tall trees, some gnarled, some graceful, a link with the prehistoric.

Nearby, across Highway 1, is a grove of Gowen cypress *(Cupressus goveniana),* which is referred to as a pygmy forest. These are small trees, rarely taller than twenty feet, and they, too, are remnants of the prehistoric. They grow here and at Pebble Beach, and nowhere else.

The most common trees around here look like the classical Christmas tree, broad at the base and pointed at the top. These are Monterey pines and Bishop pines. They are similar in appearance, though the Bishop pine is slightly more bluish in color, and its needles grow in twos rather than in threes.

From the cliffs, it is possible to spot California brown pelicans diving for fish. Around 1970, this once-common bird was a threatened species because DDT, a chemical that was widely used as a pesticide after World War II, had gotten into the food chain and into the tissues of the pelicans. The result was disasterous. It made the shells of their eggs so thin that the shells broke before the eggs could hatch.

The birds had already suffered a setback when the sardines disappeared. Evidently, pelicans are fond of sardines, for when the sardines vanished, the pelicans abandoned their nesting grounds on a nearby island. Today they hatch their young on an island near Santa Barbara, and on islands and in mangrove swamps around Baja California. DDT has diminished in the food chain, and the pelicans are making a comeback.

Perhaps the most constant threat to the pelican is the casual fisherman. The pelican will go after a baited hook, which can lead to a torn pouch or to a pelican entangled in thirty-pound test. The bird may die of infection or starvation. Signs posted on piers around Monterey Bay tell fishermen how to reel in a hooked pelican and how to cut the hook away without further injuring the bird; the problem, unfortunately, seems to be that common.

Other birds that have been driven nearly to extinction and are now protected are the peregrine falcon and the California condor. The falcon is an absolutely stunning bird, amazing to watch as it dives at speeds of up to two hundred miles an hour to yank smaller birds out of the sky. The falcon's eyesight is tremendous, equivalent to you reading this page from a distance of three hundred yards. Fierce and fast, the falcon is unmatched as an aerial predator. Yet DDT almost did it in.

This is true as well for the California condor, almost gone because of DDT. Condors are huge birds with a wing span of up to ten feet, and they are vultures. Anyone who has witnessed vultures working over a carcass knows that these birds can be exceptionally unattractive. They tear at the dead flesh, pick over the bones, and now and then erupt in great wing-flapping displays, extending their long necks to peck savagely at their competitors. But in removing dead animals from the land, the condor provides a service. And it is amazing to watch them soar at altitude, seeming never to flap a wing as they dip and circle and ride gracefully on the thermals for hours. Condors were esteemed as deities, as symbols of immortality, by the Native Americans. These birds are making a comeback by inches through intervention programs which raise the birds in captivity, with the ultimate intention of reintroducing them to the wild.

The mammals most often seen along the coast are sea lions and seals. *Lobo* is the Spanish word for wolf, and "sea wolf" is English for the name the Spanish gave the sea lion. The Spanish gave Point Lobos its name because there were so many sea lions on the shores and rocks. The sea lions share their territory with seals, another species that was once on the brink of extinction, hunted almost to death. They are now protected and are making a strong comeback.

Probably the cutest, most adorable little animal anyone has ever seen anywhere is the sea otter. Otters seem to have fun all the time. They pop up to the surface, dart around, and chase one another. They will swim on their backs with a rock balanced on their stomachs, to crack open the shells of mollusks.

When the Spanish arrived in California, sea otters were thick in the water. They were all over San Francisco Bay and ranged to Alaska. The Russians in particular hunted them for their beautiful glossy coats, and many otters ended up as hats on Russian ladies and gentlemen. So many thousands of otters were reduced to headwear that for some time in the twentieth century the little creatures were believed to be extinct. But then, to the surprise of many who had been looking for them and had given up hope of finding any, the otter reappeared. Today, the otter ranges from Morro Bay to Monterey Bay. Harmless and lovable as they are, otters still have enemies. Fishermen catch them in nets and kill them by accident or by intent. Fishermen have blamed otters for the diminished number of abalone along the coast. Yet, for thousands of years, otters and abalone lived in balance, with plenty of each in the water. Not until recently have abalone thinned out so dramatically, and it happened at a time when the otters' numbers were greatly diminished. Another danger to the otter is the oil spill. When covered by oil, the otter's coat loses its capacity to insulate, and the animal dies of exposure. Another enemy of the otter, as well as of the seal and sea lion, is the great white shark.

The waters between the Farallon Islands and Monterey Bay seem to be popular among the great whites. No one knows why, but many guess that because ships going in to San Francisco have for years dumped organic refuse over the side, the sharks are around to clean it up. These animals can grow to be as big as automobiles, and they range along the coast because that is where they can make a meal of their favorite foods: seals, sea lions, and otters. Increasingly, great whites have attacked surfers, who—like the seals, sea lions, and otters—paddle along the surface near the shore. Little is known about what motivates an attack, but attacks on humans seem to be accidental. They attack and let go, as if they realize they have made a culinary blunder. A surfboard with a huge chunk bitten out of it inspires appreciation for the power of these animals. And the little sea otter is hardly a match for them.

Perhaps the most famous creatures in the waters off Point Lobos, the ones most people want to see, are the whales. There was a time not too long ago when all that most people knew about whales was that Jonah was swallowed by one and Ahab was killed by one. On a summer afternoon in the early 1960s, when a whale was spotted near shore at Santa Cruz, people cleared the water in a panic. And they stayed clear of it long after the whale had gone. Today, people stand along the shore or go out in boats to watch them. The whales are appreciated for what they are, gentle, fascinating, enormous animals, the largest animals that have ever lived on the planet. Numerous varieties of whales swim in the ocean near here—blues, fins, humpbacks—but the ones most often noticed are the grays. Beginning in November, they can be seen swimming southward on their way to Baja for the winter. They are lumbering giants and move through the water as if in slow motion. To see them sounding, spouting water through their blow holes—particularly from a low angle on the beach—gives the impression of watching some huge, impossible geyser rising from the sea.

The commercial hunting and killing of whales is now banned by most nations, with a few disturbing exceptions. To watch these animals roll across the surface of the water, with their young traveling along beside them, to look into their eyes and see the glint of an understanding consciousness makes one wonder how men could ever have hunted and killed them, and how any could continue to do so. The whales, too, once threatened, are making a strong comeback.

Another fairly large animal roaming around here is the mountain lion. It once ranged freely up and down the state, but now the lion survives in pockets between Morro Bay and northern Big Sur, possibly making forays around Point Lobos. In the nineteenth century, ranchers and farmers killed vast numbers of mountain lions. Because of a bounty paid on them between 1907 and 1963, thousands were killed. In Monterey County alone, some six hundred of the big cats were killed. Many believed the mountain lion was extinct. But then signs of them showed up, tracks mostly, for they are extremely shy and few people have ever seen one. Now they are protected, and their numbers seem to be increasing. There are reports from people who live in and around the mountains that sometimes at night the lions can be heard making low, whistling calls to one another.

■

▲ Between meals of squid, octopus, and other sea creatures, harbor seals bask on rocks near the shore. ▶ This cove at Point Lobos, where Robert Louis Stevenson enjoyed hiking, was perhaps an inspiration for some of the scenes in *Treasure Island* and *Kidnapped*. ▶ ▶ A legion of Brandt's cormorants occupy Bird Island off the coast of Point Lobos. The flowers in the foreground are yarrow, known locally as lizard tails.

◄ China Cove at Point Lobos was the site of a Chinese fishing village in the nineteenth century. Here, Chinese immigrants were smuggled into the state after the Chinese Exclusion Act of 1882. It is likely, too, that bootleg liquor was landed here in the 1920s.
▲ Rock lies against rock on Weston Beach, once known as Pebbly Beach. It was renamed after the photographer Edward Weston, through efforts led by Ansel Adams.

▲ In shallows off Point Lobos, a snowy egret waits with beak poised for a fish it can stab or stun. ▶ Thick with age, gnarled and twisted by the elements, the life of this dead Monterey cypress might have spanned more than one hundred years.

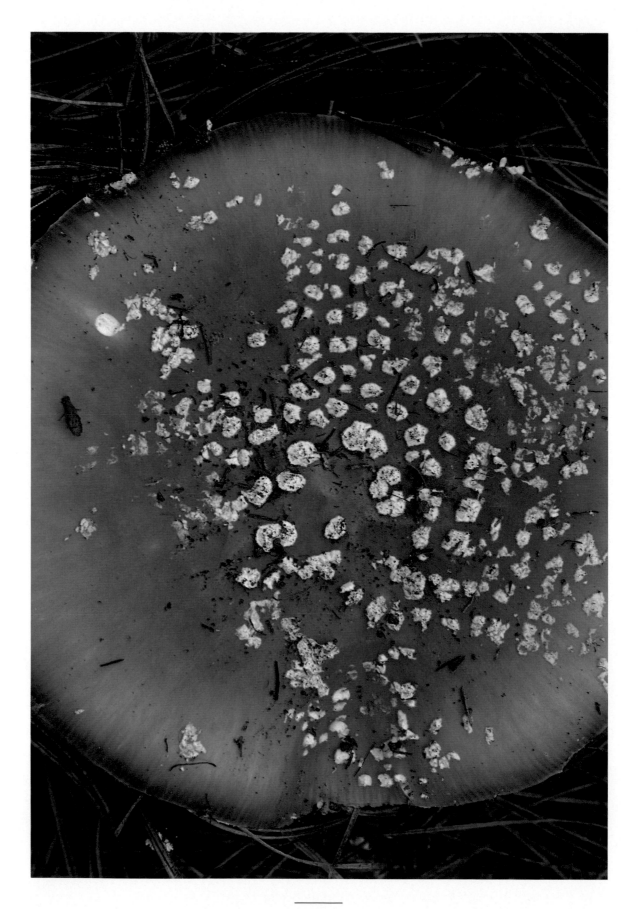

◄ The *Amanita muscaria* grows in the region's woodlands. Though deer can eat them, these vividly colored mushrooms are deadly to humans. ▲ A fearsome predator of the air, a Harris hawk has just fed on a rabbit at Point Lobos.

▲ These Monterey cypress at Bluefish Cove, on the northern shore of Point Lobos, and those at Pebble Beach are the only native groves of Monterey cypress in the world.   ▶ Seen from across Cypress Cove, Big Dome rises higher than two hundred feet and marks the highest elevation on Point Lobos.

◄ Excavation beneath the floor of Whaler's Cabin, built by the Chinese in 1851, has uncovered various artifacts that trace the cabin's history back to its earliest occupants. It now serves as a museum, which is operated by the Point Lobos Natural History Association. ▲ A mule deer and her fawn are on the alert after being interrupted while grazing among the cypress at Point Lobos.

▲ The rocky soil and cool fogs of Point Lobos are the perfect habitat for groves of Monterey cypress. That same rocky soil and those same cool fogs have combined to create some of the most spectacular scenic vistas in the world.